WHO IS YOUR GUARDIAN ANGEL?

Who Is Your Guardian Angel?

VERONIQUE JARRY

WARNER BOOKS

A Time Warner Company

Warner Books, Inc., 1271 Avenue of the Americas, New York, NY 10020
Visit our Web site at http://warnerbooks.com

 A Time Warner Company

Printed in the United States of America
First Printing: December 1998

10   9   8   7   6   5   4   3   2   1

Library of Congress Cataloging-in-Publication Data
Jarry, Veronique.
    Who is your guardian angel? / Veronique Jarry.
        p.   cm.
    ISBN 0–446–67385–4
    1. Guardian angels.   I. Title.
BL477.J38   1998
291.2' 15—dc21   98-17657
                                                          CIP

Book design by Ralph Fowler
Cover design by Elaine A. Groh
Cover illustration by Jill Karla Schwartz

TO MY FATHER, ALWAYS WITH ME
TO ANTHONY, FOR HIS FAITH AND SUPPORT

*Thanks to my mother and Michele for their great ideas,
to Olivier my greatest supporter, and to all the special people in my life, family
and friends, who gave me their help and support.*

*And I will never be able to thank John enough for his patience,
his guidance, and his lucky hand!*

Contents

Introduction   *viii*
Family Tree of Guardian Angels   *ix*
Calendar of Guardian Angels   *xi*

   I. Family of the Seraphim   1

  II. Family of the Cherubim   19

 III. Family of the Thrones   37

 IV. Family of the Dominations   55

  V. Family of the Powers   73

 VI. Family of the Virtues   91

 VII. Family of the Principalities   109

VIII. Family of the Archangels   127

 IX. Family of the Angels   145

Introduction

We all have our weaknesses and our strengths. Our Guardian Angel is here to help us overcome our weaknesses and discover our true talents.

The ancient manuscripts from all the main religions tell us of the existence of Guardian Angels. They are always here among us! They are the link between humans and Heaven.

Just like a super "bodyguard," there is someone here to help you, someone assigned to you at your birth with this sole purpose. Your Guardian Angel wants to guide you and protect you, and has given you talents that you might not even know about!

The purpose of this guide is to help you to find out more about your Guardian Angel, yourself, the people around you, and how to improve your life.

You have gifts that you can use, once you find out who your Guardian Angel is!

Family Tree of Guardian Angels

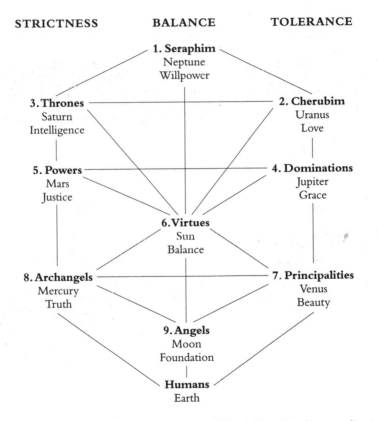

STRICTNESS   BALANCE   TOLERANCE

1. Seraphim
Neptune
Willpower

3. Thrones
Saturn
Intelligence

2. Cherubim
Uranus
Love

5. Powers
Mars
Justice

4. Dominations
Jupiter
Grace

6. Virtues
Sun
Balance

8. Archangels
Mercury
Truth

7. Principalities
Venus
Beauty

9. Angels
Moon
Foundation

Humans
Earth

There are seventy-two Guardian Angels: nine families of eight Guardian Angels each. Each family is led by a Prince-Archangel and, like all families, has specific characteristics common among its members.

SERAPHIM	Prince-Archangel: Metatron
CHERUBIM	Prince-Archangel: Raziel
THRONES	Prince-Archangel: Zaphkiel
DOMINATIONS	Prince-Archangel: Zadkiel
POWERS	Prince-Archangel: Camael
VIRTUES	Prince-Archangel: Raphael
PRINCIPALITIES	Prince-Archangel: Haniel
ARCHANGELS	Prince-Archangel: Mikael
ANGELS	Prince-Archangel: Gabriel

CALENDAR OF GUARDIAN ANGELS

JANUARY

1/1 to 5	1/6 to 10	1/11 to 15	1/16 to 20	1/21 to 25	1/26 to 30
NEMAMIAH (Archangels)	IEILAEL (Archangels)	HARAHEL (Archangels)	MITZRAEL (Archangels)	UMABEL (Archangels)	IAHHEL (Archangels)

FEBRUARY

1/31 to 2/4	2/5 to 9	2/10 to 14	2/15 to 19	2/20 to 24	2/25 to 29
ANNAUEL (Archangels)	MEHRIEL (Archangels)	DAMABIAH (Angels)	MANAKEL (Angels)	EIAEL (Angels)	HABUIAH (Angels)

MARCH

3/1 to 5	3/6 to 10	3/11 to 15	3/16 to 20	3/21 to 25	3/26 to 30
ROCHEL (Angels)	JABAMIAH (Angels)	HAIAIEL (Angels)	MUMIAH (Angels)	VEHUIAH (Seraphim)	JELIEL (Seraphim)

APRIL

3/31 to 4/4	4/5 to 9	4/10 to 14	4/15 to 20	4/21 to 25	4/26 to 30
SITAEL (Seraphim)	ELEMIAH (Seraphim)	MAHASIAH (Seraphim)	LELAHEL (Seraphim)	ACHAIAH (Seraphim)	CAHETHEL (Seraphim)

MAY

5/1 to 5	5/6 to 10	5/11 to 15	5/16 to 20	5/21 to 25	5/26 to 31
HAZIEL (Cherubim)	ALADIAH (Cherubim)	LAUVIAH (Cherubim)	HAHAIAH (Cherubim)	IEIAZEL (Cherubim)	MEBAHEL (Cherubim)

JUNE

6/1 to 5	6/6 to 10	6/11 to 15	6/16 to 21	6/22 to 26	6/27 to 7/1
HARIEL (Cherubim)	HAKAMIAH (Cherubim)	LAUVIAH (Thrones)	CALIEL (Thrones)	LEUVIAH (Thrones)	PAHALIAH (Thrones)

JULY

7/2 to 6	7/7 to 11	7/12 to 16	7/17 to 22	7/23 to 27	7/28 to 8/1
NELCHAEL (Thrones)	IEIAIEL (Thrones)	MELAHEL (Thrones)	HAHUIAH (Thrones)	NITHAIAH (Dominations)	HAAIAH (Dominations)

AUGUST

8/2 to 6	8/7 to 12	8/13 to 17	8/18 to 22	8/23 to 28	8/29 to 9/2
IERATHEL (Dominations)	SEEHIAH (Dominations)	REIIEL (Dominations)	OMAEL (Dominations)	LECABEL (Dominations)	VASARIAH (Dominations)

SEPTEMBER

9/3 to 7	9/8 to 12	9/13 to 17	9/18 to 23	9/24 to 28	9/29 to 10/3
IEHUIAH (Powers)	LEHAHIAH (Powers)	CHAVAKIAH (Powers)	MENADEL (Powers)	ANIEL (Powers)	HAAMIAH (Powers)

OCTOBER

10/4 to 8	10/9 to 13	10/14 to 18	10/19 to 23	10/24 to 28	10/29 to 11/2
REHAEL (Powers)	IHIAZEL (Powers)	HAHAHEL (Virtues)	MIKAEL (Virtues)	VEVALIAH (Virtues)	IELAHIAH (Virtues)

NOVEMBER

11/3 to 7	11/8 to 12	11/13 to 17	11/18 to 22	11/23 to 27	11/28 to 12/2
SEALIAH (Virtues)	ARIEL (Virtues)	ASALIAH (Virtues)	MIHAEL (Virtues)	VEHUEL (Principalities)	DANIEL (Principalities)

DECEMBER

12/3 to 7	12/8 to 12	12/13 to 16	12/17 to 21	12/22 to 26	12/27 to 31
HAHAZIAH (Principalities)	IMAMIAH (Principalities)	NANAEL (Principalities)	NITHAEL (Principalities)	MEBAHIAH (Principalities)	POIEL (Principalities)

Everyone is assigned a Guardian Angel at birth. Your Angel will protect you for your entire lifetime. Your date of birth determines who your Guardian Angel is.

Each Guardian Angel governs five zodiac degrees of the year, or five days. If you are born during these five days, this is your Angel. For example, if you are born March 22, your Guardian Angel is Vehuiah, the Angel of March 21 to 25 (see Calendar of Guardian Angels). And just as your zodiac gives you certain characteristics, so does your Guardian Angel.

Your Angel receives his powers from two sources. He represents the heavenly powers of his Prince-Archangel, the leader of his family, and the influence from the zodiac degrees that he governs.

Guardian Angels are here to help. They are sent to use their divine powers to help us with our human and material problems. They are good, and they will always listen and help. So you should never hesitate to talk to your Angel, just like a best friend! Your own Guardian Angel is always available for your requests.

Fill yourself with love, open the best part of yourself, and think about him with your heart. You can communicate with your Angel anytime, any day. You can also ask for the help of other Guardian Angels, if their powers are more appropriate to your needs. In this case, there are specific days to communicate with them:

Family of Virtues:	Sunday
Family of Angels:	Monday
Family of Powers:	Tuesday
Family of Archangels:	Wednesday
Family of Dominations:	Thursday
Family of Principalities:	Friday
Family of Thrones:	Saturday
Family of Cherubim:	Every day
Family of Seraphim:	Every day

Now, find out who your Guardian Angel is!

**Everything is possible
when you act with your Guardian Angel!**

I

FAMILY OF THE

Seraphim

PRINCE-ARCHANGEL: METATRON
PLANET: NEPTUNE

Characteristics of this family:

WILLPOWER

Source of life and willpower
Intellect and thoughts
Brilliance
This family is the closest to God.

Vehuiah

FIRST ANGEL OF THE SERAPHIM

Vehuiah is the Angel of

Steve McQueen

Elton John

Timothy Dalton

George Benson

Joan Crawford

Arturo Toscanini

Anthony Van Dyck

Moses Malone

Vehuiah

For persons born March 21 to 25

His protégés? You just can't stop them . . . they have life within life. They carry inside the fire of life, the energy to create.

VEHUIAH governs the first rays of the Sun. He is so radiant that his protégés are loaded with energy and can succeed in anything they undertake, especially new endeavors!

VEHUIAH will help his protégés to appease anger and to be wise. They can succeed at the most difficult tasks. They can achieve anything and beat records. They have the inner energy to get over hardship. They have a sharp and bright intelligence. They are very clear-minded toward themselves and toward traps and trickery. Courageous, direct, and dynamic, they can be very persuasive.

They will be particularly talented in arts and sciences. Not selfish, they have big hearts. They will be deeply loved, and the feelings will be complete and intense.

Jeliel

SECOND ANGEL OF THE SERAPHIM

Jeliel is the Angel of

Sandra Day O'Connor	Francisco Goya
John Tyler	Raphael
Cyrus Vance	Diana Ross
Tennessee Williams	Tracy Chapman
Vincent Van Gogh	Eric Clapton

Jeliel

For persons born March 26 to 30

JELIEL governs the destiny of kings and high dignitaries. He grants victory to those unjustly attacked. He helps to obtain the obedience of others, and to appease rebellion.

JELIEL helps his protégés to be noble and fair. Their intelligence will control their instincts, so that they can dominate what is inferior within themselves, thus allowing them to live with higher values. Their moral values will allow them to give constructive judgments and impartial advice. They will be able to solve any conflicts or disagreements, and bring order where there was chaos.

His protégés can also be quite idealistic. They will have good sense and quiet strength, and they will know how to persuade. Responsible, independent and loyal, they will also have the talent to materialize what is in their imagination. They can be successful in justice, and in constructive or creative activities.

JELIEL also inspires sentimental passion. He helps his protégés to have peace in their love life and to experience marital fidelity. They will be respected, with faithful love.

Sitael

THIRD ANGEL OF THE SERAPHIM

Sitael is the Angel of

Hans Christian Andersen

René Descartes

Alec Guinness

Jane Goodall

Marvin Gaye

Debbie Reynolds

Marlon Brando

Eddie Murphy

Alec Baldwin

Donald Sutton

Sitael

For persons born March 31 to April 4

Follow your ideas, you have the talent to make it happen!

SITAEL rules nobility, and destroys adversity. SITAEL will help his protégés to overcome any type of adversity. Lucid, pragmatic, and hardworking, they will be able to successfully materialize all of their ideas, and solve the materialistic worries of life!

What more? Hope. Hope not only for themselves, but also for people around them. SITAEL helps his protégés to live with truth and to defend truth, to keep to their word, and to do anything to be helpful to others. They will bring hope to those in need. Sincere and honest, they will be perfect for arbitration. They will have an impartial judgment and will be able to reconcile adverse parties.

SITAEL also protects against weapons and wild animals.

Elemiah

FOURTH ANGEL OF THE SERAPHIM

Elemiah is the Angel of

Colin Powell

Francis Ford Coppola

Herbert von Karajan

Harry Houdini

Bette Davis

Billie Holiday

Paul Robeson

Spencer Tracy

Jacques Brel

Elemiah

For persons born April 5 to 9

ELEMIAH governs voyages and maritime expeditions. He helps his protégés to make useful discoveries, to be industrious, and to be involved in lucky endeavors. In other words, he will help them to find the way to success and power! He grants his protégés the talent to fix a situation. When a situation is not working right, they will discover the mistake and know how to change it.

They will make the right professional choices for themselves and others, and will know when to change direction in business. Magnetic and energetic, they will find the right associates, and ELEMIAH will help them to get over worries and stress, and to discover traitors. Hardworking and strong-minded, they are also imaginative.

They will enjoy traveling, and they will receive the protection of ELEMIAH while traveling. Quite convenient!

Mahasiah

FIFTH ANGEL OF THE SERAPHIM

Mahasiah is the Angel of

Thomas Jefferson

Omar Sharif

Matthew Perry

F. W. Woolworth

Charles Evans Hughes

Samuel Beckett

Ellen Goodman

Loretta Lynn

Joseph Pulitzer

Pete Rose

Mahasiah

For persons born April 10 to 14

The pillars!

MAHASIAH grants his protégés a tremendous moral strength that nothing can destroy! They are born leaders, strong-willed and powerful. Yet they want to create harmony around them. MAHASIAH can assist them in finding a balance, by helping them to live in peace with everyone.

His protégés will carry moral and material wealth, and have access to fame and fortune! Persuasive and daring, they will also know how to be diplomatic. They will be courageous, strong and responsible. Reliable, they will get over hardship and go on with life.

MAHASIAH will help his protégés to learn very easily, and they will have access to higher sciences (philosophy, esoteric, artistic . . .). They will be very intelligent and knowledgeable. Pleasant and jovial, they are charmers. They know how to express themselves and naturally become the center of attention.

They love life and all its pleasures, including romance!

Lelahel

SIXTH ANGEL OF THE SERAPHIM

Lelahel is the Angel of

Leonardo da Vinci

Paloma Picasso

Claudia Cardinale

Jessica Lange

Bessie Smith

George Cadbury

P. W. Pillsbury

Wilbur Wright

Charlie Chaplin

Lelahel

For persons born April 15 to 20

Short and sweet . . . Venus is in charge!

LELAHEL governs love, art, science, fame, and fortune. LELAHEL will enlighten and improve anything: health, love, creation, material matters. His protégés are granted talent and can be very successful in arts and sciences. They will be able to invent, create, or discover. In any case, they can reach fame and fortune and can become famous through their work or their actions. But beware of illegal means or excessive ambition!

They are strong-willed, and LELAHEL will help them to be fair and accepting. Honorable and responsible, they can excel in many skills. They will be stable in situations of crisis of any kind, and vigorous.

Healthy and talented, they are also granted love! Kind, generous, and comforting, they can be greatly loved and be happy.

Achaiah

SEVENTH ANGEL OF THE SERAPHIM

Achaiah is the Angel of

J. Robert Oppenheimer

William Shakespeare

Charlotte Brontë

Guglielmo Marconi

Emmanuel Kant

Ella Fitzgerald

Jack Nicholson

Shirley Temple

Shirley MacLaine

Barbra Streisand

Al Pacino

Achaiah

For persons born April 21 to 25

ACHAIAH governs patience and the discovery of the secrets of nature.

His protégés are granted a sharp intelligence and a deep sense of comprehension. ACHAIAH wants them to have the desire to learn, to understand, to analyze, and this will lead to many discoveries. It is a work of patience, and ACHAIAH will help them to be patient.

They are very intelligent, and have an analytical mind that allows them to understand everything, and to grasp the right ideas or the right solution. They will want to learn useful subjects, and can discover new ideas, new concepts, or new art techniques. ACHAIAH will help them to find what is of primary importance, even if it is hidden by a facade, even if it is in the tiniest form. Their intelligence will constantly be challenged to go beyond preconceived ideas, or established ways of thinking. Organized and down to earth, they can succeed at any difficult tasks, and are talented in communication.

They will be caring and protective, and will like to be around intelligent people.

Cahethel

EIGHTH ANGEL OF THE SERAPHIM

Cahethel is the Angel of

Ulysses S. Grant

James Monroe

William Randolph
Hearst

Samuel Morse

John James Audubon

Charles Richter

Willie Nelson

Jerry Seinfeld

Michelle Pfeiffer

Eugène Delacroix

Duke Ellington

Cahethel

For persons born April 26 to 30

Certainly blessed and lucky!

CAHETHEL rules over agriculture and fertility of crops. CAHETHEL also gives his strong blessing and protection, therefore, everything will turn out for the best for his protégés. He keeps evil spirits away! He helps his protégés to be aware of God, and as long as they appreciate their blessing, they will be productive.

They will appreciate spending time in the country. They can of course work in agriculture, or any activities relating to agriculture. But in any field, they can be involved in many businesses, with productive results! They are dynamic and have the spirit and the liveliness to get over any obstacles. They have a natural talent for communication. They can be successful in expressing themselves verbally or in writing. They can reach high social levels with their work.

Protective and independent, they are also the soul of a home, and will know just how to make it harmonious. With the help of CAHETHEL, they will be able to find the right balance between work and family.

II

FAMILY OF THE

Cherubim

PRINCE-ARCHANGEL: RAZIEL
PLANET: URANUS

Characteristics of this family:

LOVE

Wisdom and love
Tolerance and kindness
Intellect and thoughts

9

Haziel

FIRST ANGEL OF THE CHERUBIM

Haziel is the Angel of

Golda Meir

Horace Mann

Audrey Hepburn

Bing Crosby

Sigmund Freud

James Brown

Benjamin Spock

Tyrone Power

Haziel

For persons born May 1 to 5

"I feel good," said James Brown. No wonder, with such a Guardian Angel!

HAZIEL grants the forgiveness of God. He will help his protégés to live with love. Gifted in love and friendship, they will generate a considerable amount of these feelings, and will receive a lot of it in return. They will have a good rapport with others and strong friendships. HAZIEL will help them to receive support and friendship from influential people, and they will be greatly appreciated by many.

They will constantly run into lucky situations, as long as they try to be diplomatic and avoid conflicts. HAZIEL will help them to keep good faith, to look for reconciliation, to be honest and keep to their word. They will be capable of keeping harmonious family ties, and will keep their promises.

Conciliatory and very sensitive, they will easily forgive others. They will have a big heart and will share their gifts with those around them. They will be calm, caring . . . and charming! They will love deeply and faithfully.

Aladiah

SECOND ANGEL OF THE CHERUBIM

Aladiah is the Angel of

Harry Truman

Fred Astaire

Rudolph Valentino

Pyotr Ilich
Tchaikovksy

Orson Welles

Thomas Lipton

Candice Bergen

Glenda Jackson

Sonia Rykiel

Aladiah

For persons born May 6 to 10

ALADIAH governs the power of healing, physically and morally. He helps his protégés to maintain good health, and to be involved in lucky endeavors.

They will be capable of turning their lives around when things go badly. ALADIAH gives them the power to change and improve their lives. They can get over their own mistakes and free themselves from the past. In life in general, privately or professionally, this regenerating power enables them to drastically improve what they do, and to find harmony. This will help them to be among the best at what they do, and therefore to succeed in their chosen field. They will be just, serious, committed to their goals, and hardworking. Yet they will also be very sensitive, which will prove to be useful not only in their profession, but also to find harmony in their life in general.

They will be respected by all!

Lauviah

THIRD ANGEL OF THE CHERUBIM

Lauviah is the Angel of

Salvador Dalí

Stevie Wonder

Thomas Gainsborough

Tom Snyder

Martha Graham

Katharine Hepburn

Gabriela Sabatini

Daphne du Maurier

Henry Fonda

George Carlin

Joe Louis

Lauviah

For persons born May 11 to 15

LAUVIAH is the protector of many celebrities. He grants victory. He influences great personages, and those who become famous through their talents.

No wonder . . . LAUVIAH grants fame, wealth, and glory!

His protégés are talented and creative. They will have a lot of imagination. They will know how to deal with influential people, befriend them, and obtain their support. They will be comfortable financially, and renowned in their field or environment. They can become very successful, and reach top levels. With so many blessings, they could become arrogant or jealous. But as long as they do not fall into these negative feelings, LAUVIAH will make sure that his protégés always retain their privileged situation.

With a good sense of humor, even ironic in some cases, they will like to play and have fun! They will have a magnetic charm. And in case it might help, LAUVIAH also protects against thunder.

Hahaiah

FOURTH ANGEL OF THE CHERUBIM

Hahaiah is the Angel of

John Paul II	Frank Capra
Malcolm X	Kathleen Sullivan
Lorraine Hansberry	Jimmy Stewart
Cher	Joe Cocker
Margot Fonteyn	Eric Gregg

Hahaiah

For persons born May 16 to 20

HAHAIAH is the refuge, the ultimate protection against adversity!

He governs thoughts and dreams and reveals hidden mysteries to humans. He stops misfortune and shows his protégés the way to better situations. Protected against bad influences, they will combine luck and love.

HAHAIAH wants his protégés to have high moral standards and pleasant manners. He helps them to be wise and spiritual. With providence on their side, these carriers of love can show their love at different levels. They can be spiritual and passionate. They will want to bring peace and comfort to those in need. Far from being selfish, they will want to give harmony and protection around them, without limits. Just and energetic, they will be dedicated and idealistic. Intense and expressive, they are also very sensitive, and can excel in expressing their feelings through art.

Ieiazel

FIFTH ANGEL OF THE CHERUBIM

Ieiazel is the Angel of

Queen Victoria of
England

Naomi Campbell

Priscilla Presley

Laurence Olivier

Arthur Conan Doyle

Bob Dylan

Miles Davis

Roseanne Cash

Plato

Ieiazel

For persons born May 21 to 25

IEIAZEL governs faithfulness, reconciliation, and friendship. Wait to see the results!

Combined, these talents create unity. His protégés can have a great role in conciliating and unifying at all levels. At a personal level, they will need union with a partner, union in which they know how to bring harmony. They can bring reconciliation between spouses, or family members, and are deeply faithful. They can make life a pleasure for people around them!

IEIAZEL will help them to have the desire to learn, and to learn anything very easily. They will have a great memory and be very clever. They will be able to achieve any difficult task. Very persuasive, they will obtain what they want from anybody. For best success, they should not use their talent to convince people to do wrong.

Their talents can be developed in many surprising ways, as can be seen in the list of his protégés!

Mebahel

SIXTH ANGEL OF THE CHERUBIM

Mebahel is the Angel of

John Wayne

Clint Eastwood

John F. Kennedy

Henry Kissinger

King Solomon

Paolo Gucci

Peter Carl Fabergé

Ian Fleming

Patrick Henry

Norman Vincent Peale

Mebahel

For persons born May 26 to 31

MEBAHEL is the Angel of justice, freedom, and truth—the exact picture of John Wayne in his movies, rushing to protect the widow and rescue the innocents!

MEBAHEL protects the innocent, and helps to regain what we have unfairly lost. Needless to say, the protégés of MEBAHEL are very special. MEBAHEL wants his protégés to defend justice and freedom, to fight for the truth, to protect the innocent. They will carry the voice of the people; they will want to help the oppressed and the needy. They will feel the pain of others. They can build the future and fight for justice. They will be carriers of human rights and can establish new rules for the well-being of people.

They will use these qualities in all aspects of their lives, regardless of their chosen field. Of course, they would be a natural in a court of law, or in the field of justice, but can also excel in any creative activity. They love the little things of life, even what seems unimportant. Protective and honorable, they are also protected against slander and thieves!

15

Hariel

SEVENTH ANGEL OF THE CHERUBIM

Hariel is the Angel of

Marilyn Monroe

Josephine Baker

Paulette Goddard

Johnny Weismuller

Ken Follett

Federico García Lorca

Thomas Hardy

Socrates

Brigham Young

John Maynard Keynes

Hariel

For persons born June 1 to 5

HARIEL governs arts and sciences.

HARIEL leads his protégés to spirituality. He wants them to have high moral standards. He helps them to purify their souls, and to live according to good values rather than lower instincts. They should use their heart and their intelligence together in their life in general, including professionally. With the influence of HARIEL, they will find the way to improve their lives. Being the Angel of arts and sciences, he will influence his protégés in these fields, and lead them to useful discoveries and new methods. Using feelings and thoughts in combination, they will have a pleasant and fulfilled life.

Quick and witty, they are inventive and know just how to solve any problem. Energetic and intelligent, they can adapt easily. They can excel in science or spirituality. They are also extremely verbal, and can become great writers or artists.

16

Hakamiah

EIGHTH ANGEL OF THE CHERUBIM

Hakamiah is the Angel of

Grace Mirabella

Thomas Mann

Judy Garland

Bonnie Tyler

Prince

Bjorn Borg

Michael J. Fox

Cole Porter

Paul Gauguin

Hakamiah

For persons born June 6 to 10

HAKAMIAH governs kings and great military leaders. He rules over iron and arsenals. He protects against traitors and grants victory. He helps people to be liberated from oppression.

HAKAMIAH wants his protégés to be honest and loyal. Direct and brave, like a knight in shining armor, they will stand up for honor, and will keep their promises. These qualities will lead them to nothing less than power! HAKAMIAH will help them to win against their enemies and to receive support from influential people.

They will be natural leaders in any field, political, professional, or private, depending on their environment. They will have the talents to change, to transform, and to create. They will have so much power that they can even change the world . . . as long as it is for the best! Daring and visionary, they will fulfill their duties. They will be very individual, and can be quite entertaining!

III

FAMILY OF THE

PRINCE-ARCHANGEL: ZAPHKIEL

PLANET: SATURN

Characteristics of this family:

INTELLIGENCE

Intelligence and understanding
Intellect and thoughts
Strictness

17

Lauviah

FIRST ANGEL OF THE THRONES

Lauviah is the Angel of

George Bush

Jacques Cousteau

David Rockefeller

Steffi Graf

Donald Trump

Joe Montana

Mario Cuomo

Dorothy Sayers

Lauviah

For persons born June 11 to 15

LAUVIAH is the Angel of knowledge.

LAUVIAH governs high sciences and marvelous discoveries. His protégés are not only intelligent and knowledgeable; they even have a sixth sense that allows them to see a different dimension. But they must use these talents in order to retain them. LAUVIAH will help his protégés to reach a higher spiritual level. They will appreciate music, philosophy, and literature. He will help them to be relieved of their worries, hurt, or disappointment. They will be able to get rid of the loads of the past and find feelings that they had lost. They should look at the matters of life not only at the surface, but in depth. There is no reason to hesitate at looking at things in depth, as this is the key to their success!

Energetic and cheerful as they are, there is no limit to the results they can achieve! One way or the other, they can push anything beyond the limits. Their knowledge and intelligence will expand, and lead them to success, fame, and fortune. If in doubt, just look at the list of his protégés!

18

Caliel

Second Angel of the Thrones

Caliel is the Angel of

St. Vincent de Paul	Dean Martin
Aung San Suu Kyi	Audie Murphy
Benazir Bhutto	Errol Flynn
Adam Smith	Paul McCartney
Kathleen Turner	Jean-Paul Sartre
Jane Russell	Blaise Pascal

Caliel

For persons born June 16 to 21

CALIEL is the Angel of truth. CALIEL helps just causes, protects the innocent, makes the truth be known, and finds the guilty ones. He also brings prompt help against adversity.

CALIEL wants his protégés to be just and honest, to look for the truth, and to be fair judges. They will be able to discern truth from lies, and will be capable of a sensitive and understanding judgment of any situation. Persistent and charismatic, they have the talent of expressing themselves and they will always find the right arguments to persuade others to their point of view. They have all the tools to reach their goals!

These talents will prove to be extremely useful, a definite gift! And they should be used with honesty, to bring justice and show the truth, both professionally and in other aspects of life. CALIEL also protects them against scandals.

Leuviah

THIRD ANGEL OF THE THRONES

Leuviah is the Angel of

E. I. Dupont

James Levine

George Orwell

Abner Doubleday

George Michael

Josephine Bonaparte

Michele Lee

Meryl Streep

Pearl S. Buck

Leuviah

For persons born June 22 to 26

LEUVIAH governs memory and intelligence. He wants his protégés to be pleasant and lively, to be simple in their behaviors and in their words. He will help them to face problems with quiet strength and patience, instead of negative or destructive reactions. They will be well balanced, pleasant, and unpretentious.

Besides their intelligence and good memory, they have a lot of imagination. They can be very creative in artistic fields, or in materializing any ideas that they have in their minds. They are very perceptive, and have the skills and the good judgment to know how to turn the right idea into reality. Imaginative and skillful, they have all the qualities to be successful and happy. Magnetic and enchanting, they can also be very romantic!

Pahaliah

FOURTH ANGEL OF THE THRONES

Pahaliah is the Angel of

Diana, Princess
of Wales

Leslie Caron

Estee Lauder

Ross Perot

Mel Brooks

Antoine de
Saint-Exupéry

Carl Lewis

Helen Keller

Lena Horne

Pahaliah

For persons born June 27 to July 1

PAHALIAH governs theology and morals. He fights to establish the truth, to have people live with morals.

PAHALIAH wants his protégés to live according to higher principles. PAHALIAH will help them to live with good morals, and overcome the lower tendencies within themselves. And their actions will reflect their ideals. When they win the battle, their life will be a picture of success! Motivated and persuasive, they will push their ideas through, all the way! They will be able to achieve what they want. Very determined, they will be demanding, with others and with themselves, yet with honesty and generosity. Interesting and intelligent, they will be focused and hardworking. They can excel in any field. As long as they have a goal, nothing will stop them from reaching it.

21

Nelchael

FIFTH ANGEL OF THE THRONES

Nelchael is the Angel of

Tenzin Gyatso

Thurgood Marshall

Louis Armstrong

Gina Lollobrigida

Cheryl Ladd

Sylvester Stallone

Tom Cruise

Geraldo Rivera

James Lofton

Franz Kafka

Nelchael

For persons born July 2 to 6

NELCHAEL rules over astronomy, mathematics, geography, and all abstract sciences. He influences savants and philosophers. He wants his protégés to be interested in studying, in seeking a higher level intellectually, spiritually, even materially.

NELCHAEL also helps against slander, bad wishes, or bad influences. In other words, any situation of disadvantage from the start can change drastically with the help of NELCHAEL! Bad luck or bad influences will go away. With this "good luck" Angel, his protégés can rise above situations of oppression or disadvantage. Everything is possible! They can succeed in any aspect of their lives.

NELCHAEL wants them to be just, faithful, and giving. They will excel in fields where they can use these qualities. Talented in sciences and philosophy, they are also very imaginative. They are sensitive and can become great artists.

22

Ieiaiel

SIXTH ANGEL OF THE THRONES

Ieiaiel is the Angel of

John Quincy Adams

Marc Chagall

Nelson Rockefeller

Pierre Cardin

Steve Wozniak

Ringo Starr

John Calvin

Arthur Ashe

Tom Hanks

Jack La Motta

Yul Brynner

Ieiaiel

For persons born July 7 to 11

IEIAIEL governs fame and financial success. He influences diplomacy and commerce. He rules over voyages and maritime expeditions, and protects against wreckage.

His protégés have a good business sense. They analyze situations very sharply. They know where and how a deal is to be made. They can impress favorably the people that they are dealing with, and persuade them. They are most certainly gifted, and they should not take advantage of their good fortune for the wrong purposes. They must be careful not to use these talents to manipulate others!

They will like commerce, and can be very industrious. Observant and inventive, they have liberal ideas and imagination. They can be very creative, and their traveling will be constructive.

23

Melahel

Melahel is the Angel of

Gerald Ford

George Washington
Carver

George Eastman

Ingmar Bergman

Rembrandt

Harrison Ford

Bill Cosby

Ginger Rogers

Barbara Stanwyck

Melahel

For persons born July 12 to 16

MELAHEL rules over waters and everything produced by the earth. He governs in particular all the medicinal plants. He helps his protégés to understand the laws of nature, the mechanisms of life. They will understand the logic between energy and creation, the link between an action and a result. They can of course be involved in health, or nature related fields, possibly natural healing. In any case, their logic of life will lead them to make the proper decision for positive results, and to create.

MELAHEL also protects against weapons, and ensures safe travel. He will help his protégés to be audacious and to have successful endeavors. They can get involved in daring endeavors, even dangerous ones, from which they will come out safe and successful. Committed and dynamic, they will be known for their honorable actions.

24

Hahuiah

Eighth Angel of the Thrones

Hahuiah is the Angel of

Nelson Mandela

Haile Selassie

John Glenn

Edgar Degas

Ernest Hemingway

Donald Sutherland

Natalie Wood

Rose Kennedy

Hahuiah

For persons born July 17 to 22

HAHUIAH gives the mercy from God. He protects against thieves and murderers. He rules over prisoners, fugitives, and outcasts. Caring and protective, he forgives them and guides them, as long as they do not make the same mistakes again!

HAHUIAH protects disadvantaged people, anyone in trouble spiritually or physically. He guides them on to the right way, the road of truth. He will help his protégés to eliminate any difficult situations and to reach harmony and fulfillment in their lives.

His protégés will like the Truth, and exact sciences. They are honest and direct, and their words and actions will be sincere. They will stand up for the truth. Courageous and active, they will find harmony in their lives, and can even lead other people onto the right way. Their willpower, combined with the motherly love of HAHUIAH, will produce great results!

IV

FAMILY OF THE

Dominations

Characteristics of this family:

GRACE

Grace and mercy
Tolerance and kindness
Desire and creation

25

Nithaiah

FIRST ANGEL OF THE DOMINATIONS

Nithaiah is the Angel of

Amelia Earhart	Stanley Kubrick
Linda Carter	Mick Jagger
Simón Bolívar	Carl Jung
Raymond Chandler	Peggy Fleming
Albert Warner	Karl Malone

Nithaiah

For persons born July 23 to 27

NITHAIAH is the poet-Angel: he delivers prophecies in rhyme!

NITHAIAH governs occult sciences and wisdom. He represents the mastering of spiritual powers, which means not only white magic, but also being able to understand the secrets of life. He reveals hidden mysteries, sometimes through dreams.

NITHAIAH will help his protégés to see the true goals of life. He will surround them with spiritual forces. The strong willpower that they will receive from him will allow them to dominate any situation!

NITHAIAH gives his protection to wise and truthful people. They will be able to master higher sciences of the mind, and can be very creative. They will love peace and solitude. And if they give precedence to the important values of life rather than their own prestige, they will lead a life of peaceful happiness. They can be very attractive, even magnetic!

26

Haaiah

SECOND ANGEL OF THE DOMINATIONS

Haaiah is the Angel of

Jacqueline Kennedy
Onassis

Henry Ford

Dag Hammarskjöld

Alexis de Tocqueville

Arnold
Schwarzenegger

Welsey Snipes

Emily Brontë

Jim Spencer

Jean Dubuffet

Ron Brown

Haaiah

For persons born July 28 to August 1

HAAIAH rules over diplomacy, politics, and ambassadors. He governs peace treaties, business contracts, and any agreements in general. He helps to win a cause, to have judges on our side.

He protects ambassadors, agents, and couriers in their mission. He will guide his protégés in their mission, in their goals. He will help them to be just and to live with truth. And as long as they are fair and truthful, he will make sure that they reach their goals, that their mission is successful.

His protégés are visionaries. They are very observant. They will have a vision, a goal. Decisive and dynamic, they will carry their ideas through and materialize their vision. They can excel in politics and economics, diplomacy, justice, or arbitration. And they are definitely talented at making speeches and expressing themselves in any form.

27

Ierathel

THIRD ANGEL OF THE DOMINATIONS

Ierathel is the Angel of

John Eisenhower

Neil Armstrong

Jack Warner

Freddy Laker

Lucille Ball

David Robinson

John Huston

Robert Mitchum

Peter O'Toole

Frédéric-Auguste
Bartholdi

Ierathel

For persons born August 2 to 6

You are among the chosen few, if you have IERATHEL for your Angel!

IERATHEL spreads light, civilization and freedom. He protects against slander and lies, enemies and unjustified aggression. He will help his protégés to spread light, justice, and freedom around them. Quick and clever, they are adaptable, yet idealistic. Determined and dignified, they are capable of being diplomatic, even elusive, to calmly but firmly reach their goals. They can have a great destiny. They will be able to create anything, even new worlds!

They will like peace and justice, sciences and arts, and will be talented for writing. IERATHEL will help them to always learn, and they will be able to succeed in absolutely any aspect of their lives, and to live with peace and happiness.

28

Seehiah

FOURTH ANGEL OF THE DOMINATIONS

Seehiah is the Angel of

Herbert Hoover	Pat Metheny
Cecil B. DeMille	Dustin Hoffman
Alex Haley	Melanie Griffith
Pete Sampras	Whitney Houston
Mstislav Rostropovich	Mata Hari

Seehiah

For persons born August 7 to 12

SEEHIAH rules over health and long life. He protects against fires, falls, diseases, handicaps, all accidents and disasters! SEEHIAH will help his protégés to go safely through the turmoil of life. He will help them to improve their health, to get over handicaps and problems.

Wisdom comes from experience, and SEEHIAH will want his protégés to learn from their problems, in order to reach a superior level. They will then be granted clear judgment and discernment. They will act with caution and think carefully and wisely before making a decision. Clever and multitalented, they are versatile and will be able to reach harmony and success in their lives. Seductive in many ways, they are fun and attractive. Their opinion will be valued, and they will be respected.

29

Reiiel

FIFTH ANGEL OF THE DOMINATIONS

Reiiel is the Angel of

Menachem Begin

Napoleon Bonaparte

Lawrence of Arabia

Princess Anne of
England

Alfred Hitchcock

Robert DeNiro

Mae West

Maureen O'Hara

Oscar Peterson

Reiiel

For persons born August 13 to 17

REIIEL governs religious feelings and meditation. REIIEL fights against the enemies of religion, or anyone acting according to the wrong principles. He protects against bad spells and evil spirits! In other words, REIIEL liberates his protégés from their enemies, whether they are visible or not. He helps his protégés to live with good values, and they will be greatly appreciated for their qualities.

They will spend a lot of energy spreading the truth. They are decisive and strong and will fight against wrong values. They will intuitively know what to do to reach their goals. Spirited and courageous, they can accomplish great things. They will be a magnet to others and can become leaders of other people. Whatever field they choose, they will act as an example and excel in their environment. Spontaneous and fun, they are talented for verbal expression. They are gifted in their rapport with other people and in social interaction.

30

Omael

SIXTH ANGEL OF THE DOMINATIONS

Omael is the Angel of

Bill Clinton

Coco Chanel

Max Factor

Malcolm Forbes

Denton Cooley

Count Basie

Roman Polanski

Robert Redford

Patrick Swayze

Wilt Chamberlain

Omael

For persons born August 18 to 22

OMAEL rules over fertility of beings. He multiplies species and perpetuates races. OMAEL also helps to fight against sadness, disappointment, and discouragement, all the negative feelings that are enemies of fertility! He can bring fertility to a couple; he gives life and health physically and morally in many ways.

He wants his protégés to be patient and courageous. Self-confident, determined, yet composed, they will reach their goals. They can become very influential in their environment.

OMAEL gives his protection to doctors, chemists, and surgeons. His protégés can excel in medicine, anatomy, or any field implying physical fertility. But fertility is creative energy, and can materialize in many ways. His protégés are very imaginative and productive, and can become great creators or artists.

31

Lecabel

SEVENTH ANGEL OF THE DOMINATIONS

Lecabel is the Angel of

Mother Theresa

Johann Wolfgang von Goethe

Jorge Luis Borges

Antoine Lavoisier

Joseph Montgolfier

Leonard Bernstein

Sean Connery

Claudia Schiffer

Patricia McBride

Lecabel

For persons born August 23 to 28

LECABEL controls vegetation and agriculture. LECABEL brings the light, which means that he grants his protégés inspiration. He wants them to follow this inspiration in a positive way.

Their comprehension of life and inspiration will produce bright ideas. They can become very spiritual and be the "speaker of God," not only in their minds, but in a practical way. They can excel in sciences, particularly in fields related to astronomy, mathematics, and geometry.

In any field, they can discover new and useful processes or concepts. They are observant and investigative, and their energy will show both intellectually or physically. They can even be quite outspoken! Caring and idealistic, they will be capable of solving the most difficult problems. They will excel in any profession that they choose, and will owe their success to nothing else than their own talent!

32

Vasariah

EIGHTH ANGEL OF THE DOMINATIONS

Vasariah is the Angel of

Ingrid Bergman

Jean-Auguste Ingres

Yvonne De Carlo

Bruce McLaren

Richard Gere

Rocky Marciano

Keanu Reeves

Jimmy Connors

Vasariah

For persons born August 29 to September 2

VASARIAH rules over justice, nobility, and magistrates. He grants the mercy of the kings. He helps to have the judges on our side when we are wrongly attacked, and to obtain the support of influential people.

VASARIAH wants his protégés to be noble in their judgment, to be just and fair. He will help them to be clear-minded and to have an objective look at situations and people. They will render a fair and honest judgment. Structured and conscientious, they can almost be inflexible once they have made their decisions. VASARIAH will help them to be pleasant and modest, and all these qualities will bring them happiness and success.

They will be granted a great memory and a definite talent for expressing themselves, verbally or otherwise. Organized and reliable, they will be successful in any field where they can use their fair judgment, or their skills for expression.

V

FAMILY OF THE

Powers

PRINCE-ARCHANGEL: CAMAEL
PLANET: MARS

Characteristics of this family:

JUSTICE

Strictness and justice
Efforts and courage
Desire and creation

33

Iehuiah

FIRST ANGEL OF THE POWERS

Iehuiah is the Angel of

King Louis XIV of France

Marquis de Lafayette

Jesse James

Ferdinand Porsche

Louis Sullivan

Daniel Burnham

Marguerite Higgins

Jane Addams

Raquel Welch

Charlie Sheen

Iehuiah

For persons born September 3 to 7

IEHUIAH is the protector of princes. He helps to find traitors and to destroy their schemes. He grants the obedience of others. And he wants his protégés to behave like princes!

He will protect what is higher and most noble within his protégés. He will help them to discover their own weaknesses, their own "traitors," and to eliminate them. He will give his protégés a lot of strength, so that they can achieve this "royal behavior," live by their higher values and remain faithful to them.

Constructive and imaginative, they are multitalented. Their imagination will lead them to create, or to build in any field. They are methodical and determined, and IEHUIAH will help them to avoid the traps and tricks on the way to their goals. Their strength and talent will bring concrete results in their work, whether it is spiritual or material, and they will enjoy all the duties associated with their work.

34

Lehahiah

SECOND ANGEL OF THE POWERS

Lehahiah is the Angel of

Cardinal Richelieu

Jessie Owens

Otis Redding

Barry White

"Colonel" Harland
Sanders

Leo Tolstoy

Maurice Chevalier

Michael Keaton

Lehahiah

For persons born September 8 to 12

LEHAHIAH protects crowned heads and makes people obedient to a higher-ranked person. He maintains harmony, good understanding, and peace between different parties. LEHAHIAH wants his protégés to work morally or materially for a superior cause or with a higher-ranked person. And they will be greatly rewarded!

Their devotion and faithfulness will bring them recognition. Efficient and organized, they will also know how to keep harmony and peace around them. They will be a tremendous help to the cause or the person that they work with. And they should work hand in hand, as their own success will derive from the success of that person, or of that cause. They will receive trust and great favors from influential people. They will be renowned for their talent and for the quality of their work.

35

Chavakiah

THIRD ANGEL OF THE POWERS

Chavakiah is the Angel of

William Howard Taft	George Chakiris
Ray Charles	Oliver Stone
B. B. King	Jean Renoir
Lauren Bacall	Agatha Christie
Claudette Colbert	David Copperfield
Peter Falk	Ettore Bugatti

Chavakiah

For persons born September 13 to 17

CHAVAKIAH is the Angel of reconciliation. He helps to receive forgiveness from the ones that we have offended. He maintains peace, harmony, and joy within family members, including cases of inheritance. He likes amiable agreements.

CHAVAKIAH will want his protégés to do this work of reconciliation around them. They might have to start within themselves. They will want to live in peace with everyone, including people with opposite interests. This work will guide them on the successful path.

Devoted and persistent, they will always need a goal, or a cause. They are tenacious and will persevere until they reach it. And CHAVAKIAH will give them the courage and the honesty to succeed in their endeavors, and in their creations. Bighearted, they will always reward the fidelity and care of the ones around them.

Menadel

FOURTH ANGEL OF THE POWERS

Menadel is the Angel of

Greta Garbo

Sophia Loren

Twiggy

Steven King

H. G. Wells

Bruce Springsteen

John Coltrane

Michael Faraday

Frankie Avalon

Menadel

For persons born September 18 to 23

MENADEL liberates prisoners, and protects against slander. He keeps exiles loyal and helps them find their land again. MENADEL will help his protégés to free themselves by reconsidering themselves and their lives. It can materialize not only as a spiritual search, but may also require them to put more efforts in their professional lives. MENADEL helps to retain a job, or financial means, and his protégés will be rewarded, as their search will lead to the discovery of spiritual treasures, and material rewards.

They will be survivors, and will enjoy life. Generous and thoughtful, they will have concern for others. They too will want to free the people around them, by helping them improve their lives. Tasteful, they are sensitive to aesthetics. They are perceptive and can be very creative.

His protégés are quite lucky to have MENADEL as their Angel; he will constantly send his providential help, materially and spiritually!

Aniel

FIFTH ANGEL OF THE POWERS

Aniel is the Angel of

Brigitte Bardot

William Faulkner

F. Scott Fitzgerald

George Gershwin

Paul VI

Marcello Mastroianni

J. L. Jericault

T. S. Eliot

Georges Clemenceau

Aniel

For persons born September 24 to 28

ANIEL represents the virtues of God. He fights against what is evil. He governs sciences and arts, and inspires the wise philosophers. His protégés have a very strong willpower!

ANIEL want his protégés to be honest and virtuous. The energy that ANIEL grants them will help them to dissolve their weaknesses. He will help them to break their routine, and improve themselves. And he will grant them victory! ANIEL wants his protégés to use their strength and willpower to be giving. Determined, they will want to inspire and help the people around them. They will be distinguished members of their environment.

They will be tasteful and sensitive. Very creative, they have a lot of imagination. Hardworking and persistent, they can become celebrities through their work. And in any case, ANIEL will make sure that they reach victory in tricky situations!

Haamiah

SIXTH ANGEL OF THE POWERS

Haamiah is the Angel of

Mahatma Gandhi

Jimmy Carter

William Rehnquist

Jerry Lewis

Deborah Kerr

Julie Andrews

Truman Capote

Graham Greene

Johnny Mathis

Vladimir Horowitz

Haamiah

For persons born September 29 to October 3

HAAMIAH protects the ones seeking the truth. He governs religion, love, and spirituality. He protects against violence, thunder, weapons, and evil spirits.

HAAMIAH wants his protégés to look for the truth. Their spiritual search will help them to live in harmony. They will find a way to combine the water and the fire within themselves. And HAAMIAH will make sure that they receive the treasures from both Heaven and Earth! Spiritually and materially, they will reach success, and have a life of peace and love.

Intense and knowledgeable, they can be very impressive. They can have a good understanding of people, of human relationships. They will know how to treat others just the right way to get their message across, and also to make them feel special. Witty and charming, they will meet their soul mate and live a great love!

Rehael

SEVENTH ANGEL OF THE POWERS

Rehael is the Angel of

Christiaan Barnard

Rutherford B. Hayes

Juan Perón

Jessie Jackson

Buster Keaton

Carole Lombard

Rehael

For persons born October 4 to 8

REHAEL rules over health and longevity. He cures diseases morally and physically. He transforms what is bad into good.

REHAEL will help his protégés to bring what is sick into health—physically, of course, but also spiritually. Anything bad will have to go away; anything good will be saved and enhanced. He will help his protégés to take responsibilities and make decisions. This process will allow them to improve any situations, to be able to solve all types of problems. And they will constantly receive providential help, spiritually and materially!

Full of life, they too will want to improve the lives of others; they will want to change things positively around them. Charming and determined, they can be quite idealistic, almost defiant. REHAEL also influences love and respect between parents and children.

Ihiazel

EIGHTH ANGEL OF THE POWERS

Ihiazel is the Angel of

Luciano Pavarotti

Henry Cavendish

Yves Montand

Eleanor Roosevelt

Art Garfunkel

Margaret Thatcher

Antoine Watteau

Ihiazel

For persons born October 9 to 13

Reach for the sky! IHIAZEL is the liberator. He frees the prisoners; he liberates people from tyranny, oppression, and all enemies.

IHIAZEL will help his protégés to free themselves from anxiety and stress. He wants them to fight their lower tendencies, to reach higher aspirations. He will liberate them from their enemies, inside and outside. With no more obstacles to their energy, they will have a very intense life!

IHIAZEL also rules over prints and books. He influences writers and artists. He inspires his protégés, and they will like reading, drawing, and all arts. Very talented, they have a lot of imagination. Observant and insightful, they are charmers and will do well socially. They can excel in arts, writing, drawing, and communication.

VI

FAMILY OF THE

Virtues

Characteristics of this family:

BALANCE

Balance and conscience
Life and willpower
Desire and creation

ᔥ 41 ᔥ

Hahahel

FIRST ANGEL OF THE VIRTUES

Hahahel is the Angel of

Dwight Eisenhower

Pierre Trudeau

Chuck Berry

Oscar Wilde

Friedrich Nietzsche

Martina Navratilova

Roger Moore

Montgomery Clift

Rita Hayworth

Hahahel

For persons born October 14 to 18

HAHAHEL rules over religion and those who spread good words. He protects against blasphemy and slander; he influences higher souls.

HAHAHEL will lead his protégés to love and wisdom. He will want their conscience to lean toward higher levels, and perceive what is really the basics of life, what is of primal importance. Having reached a fair judgment of what is essential, his protégés will not necessarily find fulfillment in this material society, including social life and obligations. They might get critical, or uncomfortable, and might even put themselves on the fringe of society. Their personal harmony is in a higher level of activities. They will find harmony in unselfish tasks. Generous, they will have a grand soul and will be unselfish. They will always try to bring comfort around them. They will have inspiration, spiritually or artistically. And HAHAHEL will help them to reach success in their goals!

42

Mikael

Second Angel of the Virtues

Mikael is the Angel of

Alfred Nobel

Catherine Deneuve

Sarah Bernhardt

Doris Lessing

John Le Carré

Michael Crichton

Franz Liszt

Pele

Mikael

For persons born October 19 to 23

MIKAEL is the Angel of mercy and righteousness. He influences kings, princes, and nobles, and makes others obedient to them. He uncovers conspiracies and those who try to destroy others. He leads the faithful to the light.

MIKAEL will enlighten his protégés, so that they understand the rules of nature, the rules of life. They will understand the order of things, and be conscientious, logical, and well balanced. They will try to provide the best environment to the people around them. They will be kind and caring.

They can act as examples for others through their life, but also through their work. They can work well as part of a team, with a higher-ranked person, or for a higher cause. Curious, they too can enlighten their surroundings, by bringing ideas, new concepts or establishing new laws. Energetic and charming, they can be very attractive. Talented in diplomacy and long distance communication, they are also protected while traveling!

43

Vevaliah

THIRD ANGEL OF THE VIRTUES

Vevaliah is the Angel of

Theodore Roosevelt

Hillary Rodham
Clinton

François Mitterand

Warren Christopher

James Cook

Richard Byrd

Pablo Picasso

Johann Strauss

Georges Bizet

Dan Gable

Julia Roberts

Jaclyn Smith

Vevaliah

For persons born October 24 to 28

VEVALIAH is the Angel of the almighty King! He rules over peace and prosperity of empires. He strengthens the power of the kings. He fights the enemies and liberates slaves.

VEVALIAH will want his protégés to fight for peace, as contradictory as it seems! They might have to fight within themselves, to reach peace inside, to reach a higher degree of love, virtue, and freedom. These feelings will influence their actions and their fights outside of themselves. As a result, their situations in any aspect of life can change drastically, from one extreme to the other, but always for the best! They will be attracted to power and glory, and VEVALIAH will grant them success if their causes are just. They will know how to fight and win their fights, and how to bring peace and prosperity to them and to others.

They will be trusted for their actions or services, and can become famous!

44

Ielahiah

FOURTH ANGEL OF THE VIRTUES

Ielahiah is the Angel of

John Adams

Warren Harding

Chiang Kai-shek

Christopher Columbus

Marie-Antoinette

Edmund Halley

Luchino Visconti

Claude Lelouch

Burt Lancaster

Stephanie Powers

Barbara Bel Geddes

Ielahiah

For persons born October 29 to November 2

IELAHIAH grants victory. He protects against weapons. He helps to have judges on our side and favorable decisions in legal suits. He grants success to positive ventures.

His protégés will have strong ideas and strong feelings. Energetic and confident, they can sometimes go overboard! IELAHIAH will grant them courage and strength. They will be brave fighters, and IELAHIAH will make sure that they already reach victory in their endeavors, as long as they are not motivated by the wrong values. Influential and powerful, they are indomitable! They will like to travel in a constructive way.

They can become celebrities with their accomplishments, even heroes who will do a lot to improve this world. They will have a life of strong emotions!

§ 45 §

Sealiah

Sealiah is the Angel of

Yitzhak Shamir	Bryan Adams
Marie Curie	Sally Field
Charles Bronson	Vivian Leigh
Roy Rogers	Monica Vitti
Billy Graham	André Malraux
Barry Newman	Albert Camus

Sealiah

For persons born November 3 to 7

SEALIAH is the universal motor. He controls vegetation and fertility. He brings life and health to anything in nature, energy to any aspect of life. He gives strength and hope to the humiliated, the deprived, and the oppressed. SEALIAH's fertile energy stimulates everything around him. He can change any situation for the best. His protégés, when in a situation of disadvantage, can see great changes in their lives.

SEALIAH can make any endeavor flourish. His protégés will have the endurance to go all the way to their goals. They will like to learn, and will have the means and talents to do so easily.

SEALIAH wants his protégés to carry the same warm energy. Curious and energetic, they will know how to stimulate those around them. They will be knowledgeable and healthy. Their endeavors will be fertile and successful.

§ 46 §

Ariel

SIXTH ANGEL OF THE VIRTUES

Ariel is the Angel of

George Patton

Fyodor Dostoyevsky

John Northrop

Martin Luther

Ennio Morricone

Ivan Turgenev

Neil Young

Grace Kelly

Margaret Mitchell

Demi Moore

Ariel

ARIEL is the Angel of revelation. He reveals the most important secrets of nature. He shows hidden treasures.

ARIEL will help his protégés to discover hidden treasures, spiritually and materially! His protégés might be able to foresee the future in their dreams. ARIEL will help them to dig out what is best within themselves, and in others as well. He wants his protégés to have a strong and subtle mind. They will have great ideas and bright thoughts. They are very perceptive, and their senses will be very sharp. They will be able to discover new ways, or have innovative ideas. These discoveries can lead to following a new path in their lives, or creating great changes in their lives.

Attractive or magnetic, they know how to seduce and persuade. They will be able to solve the most difficult of problems, and will make enlightened and cautious decisions. They will be able to enrich their lives spiritually and materially.

Asaliah

SEVENTH ANGEL OF THE VIRTUES

Asaliah is the Angel of

King Hussein of Jordan

Jawaharlal Neru

Boutros Boutros-Ghali

Bernard Montgomery

Erwin Rommel

Whoopi Goldberg

Robert Louis Stevenson

Claude Monet

Lee Strasberg

Rock Hudson

Asaliah

For persons born November 13 to 17

ASALIAH rules over justice and makes the truth be known.

ASALIAH wants his protégés to be honest and virtuous. He protects against immoral behaviors and scandals! He helps his protégés to elevate their souls, to live with justice and truth. He will enlighten their intellect, and inspire great ideas. They will know what is right and what is wrong, what is truth from what is lies. Clear-minded and courageous, they will be fair and will defend what is just.

Measured and helpful, they will get very involved in defending the cause or the project that they have chosen. Knowledgeable, they will also have an excellent memory. They will find solutions for problems, and apply them. Observant and thorough, they will be able to change any situation. They will materialize their ideas with authority. In short, they are assured of the success of their projects!

Mihael

EIGHTH ANGEL OF THE VIRTUES

Mihael is the Angel of

Charles de Gaulle

Voltaire

Indira Gandhi

Jodie Foster

Meg Ryan

Gene Tierney

Linda Evans

Charles Schultz

Chester Gould

René La Salle

Thomas Cook

Calvin Klein

Boris Becker

Mihael

For persons born November 18 to 22

MIHAEL controls conjugal fidelity and friendship. He rules over fertility and the reproduction of living beings.

MIHAEL wants his protégés to have peace and strength in their relationships. They will have a good rapport with the other sex in general. They can have a deep and faithful love and friendship with their mate. It is important for their personal balance that they find this relationship. They will have fruitful rapport with others, which will create strong friendships, and also with different generations, such as their children and other family members.

Very active, they will be extremely productive and creative professionally, artistically, or in any field that they have chosen. They are intuitive and can have premonitions about the future. Kind and generous, they have a lot of humor and a lot of charm! They draw a lot of attention socially. MIHAEL also wants his protégés to travel a lot, and to taste all of the pleasures of life, spiritual and material.

VII

FAMILY OF THE

Principalities

PRINCE-ARCHANGEL: HANIEL
PLANET: VENUS

Characteristics of this family:

BEAUTY

Beauty and victory
Tolerance and kindness
Link between Heaven and Earth

§ 49 ❧

Vehuel

FIRST ANGEL OF THE PRINCIPALITIES

Vehuel is the Angel of

John XXIII

Joe DiMaggio

Tina Turner

Little Richard

Henri de Toulouse-Lautrec

Dale Carnegie

Rudy Tomjanovich

Jimi Hendrix

Vehuel

For persons born November 23 to 27

VEHUEL shines like a sun! VEHUEL governs great personages, people of virtue and talent.

He wants his protégés to develop their virtues. They will have to discover their true personality and their real talents, and this will change their lives! VEHUEL will enhance their natural qualities. Energetic and free-spirited, they will enjoy everything, and everything will be beautiful and exciting for them. They are so sensitive that they will pick up the beauty of anything in life, and they will shine just like VEHUEL does.

VEHUEL will protect his protégés against sadness and annoyance. He will make sure that his protégés get over any adversity that they might encounter. They will get thoroughly involved in any task they choose, and will be able to accomplish anything. They will share their dynamism with everyone around. Generous and loyal, they will be very much appreciated by others for their qualities and their actions.

50

Daniel

SECOND ANGEL OF THE PRINCIPALITIES

Daniel is the Angel of

Winston Churchill	Bette Midler
Mark Twain	Tracy Austin
Jonathan Swift	Claude Lévi-Strauss
Woody Allen	Edwin Meese III
Maria Callas	

Daniel

For persons born November 28 to December 2

DANIEL rules over justice, lawyers, and judges. DANIEL is also the Angel of mercy and comfort.

His protégés will have good and fair judgment. DANIEL will inspire them when they are in doubt, when they do not know what to decide. They will sharply and objectively judge situations and people, and will be talented at conciliation. He will give them the moral strength to turn situations around, and will also give them motivation and courage even if they are at the end of their rope. He wants his protégés to live by these principles, and to inspire others as well. They will comfort those in need, and bring them new hope for life.

Lucid and naturally gifted with eloquence, they can portray their judgment through humor, and can of course succeed in the field of law. They will have a taste for literature. Dynamic and vibrant, they will be very industrious and will excel in business.

51

Hahaziah

THIRD ANGEL OF THE PRINCIPALITIES

Hahaziah is the Angel of

Walt Disney;
needless to say more!

Hahaziah

For persons born December 3 to 7

HAHAZIAH governs chemistry and physics. He reveals the greatest secrets of nature and medicine. He is the ultimate medicine man. Like a magician, he brings back physical or moral health. He wants his protégés to elevate their souls, to discover wisdom.

HAHAZIAH represents a lot of kindness. Kindness and sincerity should be the leaders of his protégés' lives. They will find harmony by making life easier and more pleasant for others, physically or morally. And they will have access to great knowledge.

His protégés will want to understand all the properties inherent in animals, plants, and minerals. They will like abstract sciences. They have a mind of their own, and in their unique way, they go for their goal without blinking. Energetic and capable, they can be gutsy and daring. They are imaginative and innovative. They can make great discoveries, and they can be very useful to society.

52

Imamiah

FOURTH ANGEL OF THE PRINCIPALITIES

Imamiah is the Angel of

Alexander Solzhenitsyn

Eli Whitney

John Milton

Gustave Flaubert

Sammy Davis Jr.

David Carradine

Frank Sinatra

Kirk Douglas

Douglas Fairbanks Jr.

Kim Basinger

Imamiah

For persons born December 8 to 12

IMAMIAH controls voyages and destroys the power of our enemies. He protects prisoners and helps them to find the way to freedom.

IMAMIAH will release his protégés from situations of oppression, or lack of freedom. He will help them to set themselves free from anything holding them back, spiritually or physically. They will be able to free themselves from their own negative feelings, which can be their first enemy. He protects those looking for truth, those who are sincere in their search. They can have a great purpose or mission in their lives, and can be very influential in their environment. They too can stand up to help people in need, prisoners of any kind.

They will be courageous and patient when confronted with problems. Brave and strong, they are energetic and intense. Whatever field they choose, they will be able to easily achieve any goals.

§ 53 ❧

Nanael

FIFTH ANGEL OF THE PRINCIPALITIES

Nanael is the Angel of

Nostradamus

Gustave Eiffel

Ludwig van Beethoven

J. Paul Getty

Jane Austen

Margaret Mead

Liv Ullmann

Lee Remick

Nanael

For persons born December 13 to 16

NANAEL rules over great sciences. He protects philosophers, ecclesiastics, professors, and people of law.

NANAEL wants his protégés to reach a higher knowledge, a higher level of the soul, an elevated spiritual level. They will be able to understand higher sciences, and will practice true justice. This higher knowledge can give them inspiration for unique types of work, different ideas, even daring pieces of work. They are visionary and imaginative, and the confidence that they will have in life in general will allow them to get involved in unique projects. Their endeavors might be philosophical, spiritual, scientific, and even artistic. Perceptive, they are very detail-oriented. Even if they appear aloof, or lost in their thoughts, they keep their goal in mind, as distant as it may be.

NANAEL will help them to appreciate privacy and peace and quiet. They will need to have a quiet place to meditate, a sanctuary to renew themselves.

Nithael

SIXTH ANGEL OF THE PRINCIPALITIES

Nithael is the Angel of

Jane Fonda	Ty Cobb
Edith Piaf	Bob Hayes
Steven Spielberg	Willy Brandt
Jean Racine	Willard Libby

Nithael

For persons born December 17 to 21

NITHAEL governs kings, emperors, and high dignitaries. He gives strength and stability to rightful empires. He gives long and peaceful lives to the princes faithful to him.

NITHAEL grants long life and mercy to his protégés. He protects against accidents and falls. He helps his protégés to retain their position, or to keep their job. He wants them to use their powers and talents to benefit others, to bring stability and prosperity around them. He wants them to be faithful to their environment. They will be trusted, known, and appreciated for their virtues.

Gifted and capable, they are persistent and very productive. They are impulsive, even indomitable. They can acquire a reputation linked to their physical abilities, or physics in general. They will be very talented in writing and verbal expression. They can be very seductive or magnetic. With kindness and concern for others, they will have a life of abundance and can reach the top of their field. They can be the king of this world, and the king of the other world!

55

Mebahiah

SEVENTH ANGEL OF THE PRINCIPALITIES

Mebahiah is the Angel of

Howard Hughes

Louis Chevrolet

Conrad Hilton

Helena Rubinstein

Isaac Newton

Anwar Sadat

Helmut Schmidt

Ava Gardner

Cab Calloway

Jimmy Buffett

Mary Higgins Clark

Hawayo Takata

Mebahiah

For persons born December 22 to 26

MEBAHIAH represents eternity. He rules over morals and religion. He helps the ones living with good morals and those who defend the truth.

MEBAHIAH is also very fertile. He brings comfort, and help in conceiving in all fields, including having children. His protégés are builders! MEBAHIAH wants them to be productive and fertile, to use their talents for good and constructive causes. They will have a tremendous moral strength, sometimes also physical strength.

They will naturally command respect. Careful and measured even when taking risks, they will be persevering and methodical. They will have visions and can go overboard to accomplish their duties. They will be known for their positive impact. They will be achievers, who can create great work, even build empires! They are among a very special class of people, whose names can become legends.

56

Poiel

Eighth Angel of the Principalities

Poiel is the Angel of

Woodrow Wilson

Andrew Johnson

Elizabeth Arden

Marlene Dietrich

Mary Tyler Moore

Gerard Depardieu

Rudyard Kipling

Louis Pasteur

Jacques Cartier

Henri Matisse

Poiel

POIEL's protégés are blessed! POIEL rules over fame, fortune, and philosophy. He grants absolutely everything!

He grants his protégés so much, in such abundance, that they will have to pass it on, giving comfort and support to others. POIEL wants them to remain modest and moderate, and their pleasant character will gain them the esteem of all.

Giving and highly capable, they can succeed in any aspect of their lives. Noble and tasteful, they will be interesting and dependable. POIEL adds life to the words of his protégés, and they can become charming, even persuasive. They will be very talented in any form of communication. They will owe their success solely to their own talents and behavior.

VIII

FAMILY OF THE

Archangels

PRINCE-ARCHANGEL: MIKAEL
PLANET: MERCURY

Characteristics of this family:

TRUTH

Strictness and truth
Glory
Formation and life

Nemamiah

FIRST ANGEL OF THE ARCHANGELS

Nemamiah is the Angel of

Konrad Adenauer

William Crowe

Jakob Grimm

Isaac Asimov

Louis Braille

Isaac Pitman

Diane Keaton

Victoria Principal

Mel Gibson

Don Shula

Nemamiah

For persons born January 1 to 5

NEMAMIAH rules over admirals and generals, and all those who engage in just causes. He liberates prisoners. NEMAMIAH also grants prosperity in all things, in all fields.

NEMAMIAH wants his protégés to have a grand soul and a noble mind. He wants them to fight for good causes. Lucid, intelligent and decisive, they have all the qualities of good fighters! They will withstand problems and fatigue with a lot of courage.

They are quite clear-minded, and their talents will make them choose the right endeavors to get involved in. They can even discover new concepts or great ideas. They will devote themselves entirely to their cause, whether it is personal or professional. Highly responsible, they will be dedicated and trustworthy. They will be generous and caring. And as long as they act with the goodness of their souls, NEMAMIAH will make sure that they win their battles!

Ieilael

SECOND ANGEL OF THE ARCHANGELS

Ieilael is the Angel of

Richard Nixon	Joan Baez
Elvis Presley	Lou Harris
Loretta Young	George Foreman
David Bowie	Simone de Beauvoir
Rod Stewart	George Balanchine
Shirley Basset	

Ieilael

For persons born January 6 to 10

IEILAEL is the Angel of iron. He rules over gunsmiths, locksmiths, ironsmiths—anyone dealing with iron. IEILAEL also helps relieve sadness and disappointment. He can cure diseases, in particular where eyes were concerned. He fights against mean people and liars.

His protégés are granted a sharp intelligence, a precise and meticulous mind. And IEILAEL wants them to be brave and honest. He will help them to react without anger or violence. They will be accepting, yet intense. They will clear-mindedly observe and analyze facts, with no preconceived ideas, and will search for the truth. Their minds work scientifically, with patience.

They will use their intelligence for a useful goal, to add something to the lives around them. They will devote every ounce of their energy to their goal. Searching and intuitive, they might have unusual interests and can be very influential in their field.

Harahel

THIRD ANGEL OF THE ARCHANGELS

Harahel is the Angel of

Martin Luther King Jr.	Horatio Alger
Alexander Hamilton	John Dos Passos
Aristotle Onassis	Martin Agronsky
Albert Schweitzer	Mario Van Peebles
Molière	Faye Dunaway
Jack London	Kirstie Alley

Harahel

For persons born January 11 to 15

HARAHEL governs treasures, archives, libraries, and public funds. He rules over printing, books, and anything related to books and intellectual broadcasting. HARAHEL is a very fertile Angel. He promotes physical fertility of course, as he can help people to have children, but also intellectual fertility.

He wants his protégés to engage in constructive intellectual activity. They will want to study and learn. And he will grant them honesty, talent, and fortune.

They will indeed have an intellectual wealth that will materialize in successful affairs. Strong-willed and committed, they will follow their calling. They will be determined to grow and reach their goal. They can have great ideals, that they will fight for with courage and pride. They can succeed in any field where they can broadcast or make public their intellectual work, or where they can use it to better the conditions of others. They will also be talented in business, in making successful deals and investments.

60

Mitzrael

FOURTH ANGEL OF THE ARCHANGELS

Mitzrael is the Angel of

Benjamin Franklin

James Watt

George Burns

Buzz Aldrin

Federico Fellini

Edgar Allan Poe

Anton Chekhov

Paul Cézanne

Sade

Dolly Parton

Cary Grant

Muhammad Ali

Joe Frazier

Mitzrael

For persons born January 16 to 20

MITZRAEL governs distinguished personages, renowned for their talent and virtues. He grants obedience from people from different ranks.

MITZRAEL brings health to the mind, and liberates those that are oppressed or persecuted. MITZRAEL wants his protégés to clean their minds, to reach higher qualities of the spirit and liberate themselves from the thoughts holding them back.

They will reach great strength mentally and physically, and can live to be very old. Their thoughts will be clear; they will have new ideas. They will be known and appreciated for their physical or intellectual talent, and for their spirit. Very individual, they will have a style of their own. They will be imaginative and creative, and can launch new ideas or new concepts. Forceful, they will know how to beat the competition, in any field that they choose.

61

Umabel

FIFTH ANGEL OF THE ARCHANGELS

Umabel is the Angel of

André-Marie Ampere

Robert Boyle

Geena Davis

Humphrey Bogart

Steve Reeves

Placído Domingo

Christian Dior

Cristobal Balenciaga

Édouard Manet

Lord Byron

Somerset Maugham

Virginia Woolf

Francis Bacon

Hakeem Olajuwon

Umabel

For persons born January 21 to 25

UMABEL has a mixture of the romantic and scientific mind! UMABEL rules over physics and astronomy and anyone related to those fields.

His protégés will have a very scientific mind, and are gifted in anything to do with physics, astronomy, astrology, and mathematics. They will also be in tune with the proper functioning of the body, including their own.

UMABEL wants his protégés to travel, and to enjoy all the honest pleasures of life. They are very sensitive, and feel deep emotions. Their passions are their motivations; they follow their heart. And they should! Their feelings will dictate the right decisions, and lead them to creative situations. They will have deep affections and great friendships. Talented and exciting, they can be very attractive and magnetic. They are romantic, with a very sensitive heart, and their love life can be quite eventful. They should be careful not to become libertines!

62

Iahhel

Sixth Angel of the Archangels

Iahhel is the Angel of

Franklin Roosevelt	Roger Vadim
Paul Newman	Lewis Carroll
Tom Selleck	Henry Stanley
Phil Collins	Mikhail Baryshnikov
Wolfgang Amadeus Mozart	Vanessa Redgrave

Iahhel

For persons born January 26 to 30

IAHHEL rules over philosophers and those who want to withdraw from worldly matters. He helps to acquire wisdom.

IAHHEL wants his protégés to rise above inconsistencies or superficial concerns. He wants them to use their talents in a wise way, to elevate their soul. As active and sensitive as they are, they can direct their energy in any field, and IAHHEL will help them to use it for positive goals. They should have an environment of peace and quiet, and solitude. This will allow them to "recharge" for the best, and to find personal harmony. And they will reach success peacefully and easily!

Strong-willed and bright, his protégés will devote themselves to their goals, and will conscientiously fulfill their duties, with pleasure. They will be known and appreciated for their modesty and their qualities. They will like to have fun, and most likely be social. They can have an intense rapport with the other sex, and can be tenderly loved.

63

Annauel

SEVENTH ANGEL OF THE ARCHANGELS

Annauel is the Angel of

Charles Lindbergh

Clark Gable

Valéry Giscard d'Estaing

Princess Stephanie of Monaco

Farrah Fawcett

James Michener

Norman Rockwell

John Ford

Franz Schubert

Stan Getz

Betty Friedan

Rosa Parks

Annauel

For persons born January 31 to February 4

ANNAUEL rules over commerce, bankers, and brokers. He handles all kinds of requests. He protects against accidents, and protects travelers. He grants good health and protects against diseases. And he grants financial protection.

Traditionally, ANNAUEL gives power to bring nations to a just, peaceful, and prosperous regime. In other words, all the gifts that his protégés receive should be used to better their lives and turn their enemies around.

ANNAUEL wants his protégés to use their gifts in a sensible way. They will have a subtle and ingenious mind. Dynamic and perfectionistic, they will pay attention to details, and can succeed in the technical arts. They will be known for being active and industrious, and can be very successful financially. Entertaining and attractive, they can be quite sophisticated. And they will be appreciated, even admired, for all these qualities.

64

Mehriel

EIGHTH ANGEL OF THE ARCHANGELS

Mehriel is the Angel of

Ronald Reagan

Charles Dickens

Jules Verne

Alice Walker

Laura Ingalls Wilder

King Vidor

François Truffaut

Bob Marley

Natalie Cole

James Dean

Jack Lemmon

Charlotte Rampling

Lana Turner

Mia Farrow

Mehriel

For persons born February 5 to 9

MEHRIEL protects professors, scholars, authors, and orators. He rules over everything related to printing, books, and images. He also protects against adversity, anger, and wild animals. MEHRIEL brings thoughts and wishes to life.

His protégés have a lot of imagination. And any wish, any thought, any idea can materialize. They will be able to explain their reasoning through pictures, writings, or speeches. And MEHRIEL wants their ideas to be aimed at instructing people, or at passing on a message. Their thoughts have a practical and productive profile, as opposed to a more abstract form of intellectualism. Inspired and intuitive, they are vibrant and natural. They will be liked for their spontaneity and their easygoing behavior.

They will be successful in any field relating to writing, imagination, and verbal expression. They can be great orators or famous authors!

IX

FAMILY OF THE

Angels

Characteristics of this family:

FOUNDATION

Balance and foundation
Formation and life
Imagination becoming reality
This family is the closest to humans.

65

Damabiah

FIRST ANGEL OF THE ANGELS

Damabiah is the Angel of

Abraham Lincoln

Thomas Edison

Chuck Yeager

Vivian Fuchs

Charles Darwin

Marc Spitz

Boris Pasternak

Georges Simenon

Richard Wagner

Gregory Hines

Burt Reynolds

Kim Novak

Damabiah

For persons born February 10 to 14

DAMABIAH rules over oceans, rivers, maritime voyages, and naval construction. He governs anything related to fishing, sailing, and water.

DAMABIAH protects against evil and bad spells and grants wisdom. His protégés have the ultimate protection against anything or anyone with ill intentions. Wisdom means love and kindness in the lives of his protégés. DAMABIAH wants them to be deeply kind and good-hearted, and nothing negative will touch them.

They might have to travel a long way, and this travel will lead them to a great discovery, a treasure. This search can be either physical or spiritual. DAMABIAH will protect them against wreckage along this voyage, and will make sure that it leads to an enriching discovery. They can, of course, excel in any field related to oceans and waters. But in any situation, DAMABIAH will ensure that their search leads to greatly improving their lives!

§ 66 §

Manakel

Manakel is the Angel of

Nicolaus Copernicus

Galileo Galilei

Alexander Volta

Michael Jordan

John McEnroe

John Travolta

Milos Forman

Amy Tan

Matt Groening

Enzo Ferrari

Charles and Louis
Tiffany

Jane Seymour

Cybill Shepherd

Manakel

For persons born February 15 to 19

MANAKEL governs vegetation and aquatic animals. He influences sleep and dreams, and helps to cure what is bad.

This family of Angels is the closest to humans, and MANAKEL understands the weaknesses of his protégés. He wants them to gather the best qualities of the body and of the soul. He will help them to improve themselves, to be kinder and more amiable if they need to be. He will bring constancy and stability in their actions. They will make good and just decisions.

With their pleasant manners, they will easily gain friendship and support from influential people. Very sensitive, even if they don't show it, they will be ingenious. Supportive and reliable, they will be perceived as the ones who assist and help. They are spirited and determined, and their practical intelligence will help them to realize the pictures that they have in mind, and they will find the obvious way to success!

Eiael

THIRD ANGEL OF THE ANGELS

Eiael is the Angel of

George Washington

Chester Nimitz

Johannes Gutenberg

Frédéric Chopin

Nina Simone

Sidney Poitier

William Du Bois

Cindy Crawford

Julius Erving

Charles Barkley

Niki Lauda

Alain Prost

Hubert de Givenchy

Eiael

For persons born February 20 to 24

EIAEL rules over changes, and longevity of life and of material things. He governs occult sciences.

EIAEL inspires the mind of his protégés, so that they can see the truth in life. He will comfort them in adversity so that they always see the positive side of any situation. They will be able to appreciate the beautiful side of all things in life.

Unselfish and giving, they will be dedicated. They will want to learn, to question, and to reconsider. EIAEL will enlighten them, so that they discover the truth in their work, in themselves, or in any situation. They will have bright ideas and insights! And he will give them strength when they are confronted with enemies, to ensure that they will not have to hide the truth. They will like comfort, peace, and quiet, and will be talented in higher sciences, astronomy, physics, and philosophy.

Habuiah

FOURTH ANGEL OF THE ANGELS

Habuiah is the Angel of

Elizabeth Taylor

Fats Domino

Buffalo Bill Cody

John Steinbeck

Ron Santo

Victor Hugo

Pierre-Auguste Renoir

David Puttnam

Vincente Minelli

Gioacchino Rossini

George Frideric Handel

Habuiah

For persons born February 25 to 29

Quite simple: the protégés of HABUIAH can reach the perfect situation, in any field of action that they have chosen! HABUIAH gives his protégés the strength and the courage to work hard in the direction that they have chosen. And this work will be fruitful. Regardless of the direction chosen, the results will be grand!

HABUIAH governs agriculture and fertility. He grants good health and cures diseases. He is very fertile, in every sense!

His protégés can have a special attraction toward nature and agriculture. In any field, their actions will be very fertile and productive. Capable and devoted, they will be vibrant. They can have a magnetic influence on others, and stimulate everyone around. They will be a fountain of life and health and will make life beautiful for those around them!

Rochel

FIFTH ANGEL OF THE ANGELS

Rochel is the Angel of

Mikhail Gorbachev

George Pullman

Alexander Graham
Bell

Glenn Miller

Perry Ellis

Jean Harlow

David Niven

Harry Belafonte

Rex Harrison

Jim Clark

Miriam Makeba

Rochel

For persons born March 1 to 5

ROCHEL governs fame, fortune, and inheritance. He rules over magistrates and lawyers. ROCHEL also brings the light to find what we have lost, or what was stolen, and to discover the thieves.

He will enlighten the mind of his protégés, so that they may find what they have lost. They might have to get rid of the burden of the past, and reconsider themselves. ROCHEL gives his protégés the strength to stop playing different roles in order to find their true self. They will discover the strength and talents that they have, and did not even suspect! These newly discovered qualities will lead them to success and personal harmony. They will reach an intensity and energy that nothing will destroy.

They are strong and bright, and ROCHEL wants them to use their talents for the proper application of the law. They will excel in the field of law, or in anything related to the customs and habits of people. Creative and productive, they are very sensitive to their environment in general, and are artistically inclined. Very imaginative, yet pragmatic, they will be loyal and dependable.

Jabamiah

SIXTH ANGEL OF THE ANGELS

Jabamiah is the Angel of

Michelangelo

Gabriel García Márquez

Andrzej Wajda

Cyrano de Bergerac

André Courrèges

Maurice Ravel

Yuri Gagarin

Davy Crockett

Cyd Charisse

Sharon Stone

Ivan Lendl

Antoine Becquerel

Jabamiah

For persons born March 6 to 10

Be thankful for the luck that you have! JABAMIAH is the almighty creator. He rules over the generation of beings, and all the phenomena of nature. He grants absolutely everything; he makes ANYTHING possible!

JABAMIAH represents the eternal fertility. He wants his protégés to regenerate themselves, to restore harmony within, by purifying their nature, and emphasizing internal values. And they will become the masters of life; they will have in their hands all creating powers!

They are very sensitive and emotional, and their mind is abstract and active. They will succeed in putting their thoughts into concrete forms of expression. Conceptual and intuitive, they will be extremely creative. Aesthetically astute, they will be very sensitive to beauty, and will carry a personal magnetism. They will be known for their genius, and respected for their talents and their philosophy. All of their endeavors will be fruitful and creative, and they will always find favorable circumstances to succeed in their goals!

Haiaiel

SEVENTH ANGEL OF THE ANGELS

Haiaiel is the Angel of

Andrew Jackson

Kemal Atatürk

Albert Einstein

Paul Ehrlich

Andrew Young

Antonin Scalia

Ruth Bader Ginsburg

Rupert Murdoch

Quincy Jones

Michael Caine

Billy Crystal

Liza Minelli

Maxim Gorky

Haiaiel

For persons born March 11 to 15

HAIAIEL grants victory and peace. He protects against ill-intentioned people, and liberates the oppressed. He rules over iron, arsenals, and military engineering.

HAIAIEL protects against any negative situation or influence. He wants his protégés to use their talents for good purposes. They will have a strong sense of justice, and will always defend just causes. Energetic, they will be granted a lot of courage. They can excel in the military, and in any case, they will lead the battles of their lives like successful generals! They are good-hearted, and will always reach victory, when they are involved in just causes.

His protégés are very lucid and clear-minded. They have visions and intuitions that they follow all the way! Quick and clever, they are progressive and determined. They are daring and courageous, and will be known for their talents and their activity. Very charismatic people!

Mumiah

EIGHTH ANGEL OF THE ANGELS

Mumiah is the Angel of

James Madison

Wyatt Earp

David Livingstone

Georg Simon Ohm

Ursula Andress

Glenn Close

Kurt Russell

Bruce Willis

Spike Lee

Pat Riley

Rudolf Nureyev

Nikolai Rimsky-
Korsakov

Mumiah

For persons born March 16 to 20

MUMIAH governs chemistry, physics, medicine, and influences health and longevity. He is the Angel of completion: he brings anything, any endeavor to a successful end!

MUMIAH is very efficient and acts with no moderation. He wants his protégés to discover the good side of life, and enjoy it. Carriers of life and health, his protégés will have intense values, and express them with the energy and intensity of MUMIAH! Very expressive, his protégés are not quiet and discreet. They are active and enthusiastic. They represent a good balance of imagination, and down to earth behavior. Persistent, they get involved and pursue their actions to the end. They can, of course, excel in medicine. But in any field, they will be able to discover the secret of happiness, and share it with the ones around them, especially ones in need. They will have the power to complete anything they start, and in all aspects of life, their endeavors will be successful!